Anger Management

Mastering Emotions: A Manual For Managing Stress, Developing Self-Belief, And Handling Life's Tough Triggers And Disagreements

(Ways To Become An Emotional Master So You Can Make Sense Of Anything)

Tommaso Leoni

TABLE OF CONTENT

So Feeling Anger Is Not "Bad"? 1

The Distinctions Between Responding And Reacting 10

The Dangers Of Getting Enraged 20

Anger And The Controll Of Anger 42

Overview 53

Anger: What Is It? 53

Different Kinds Of Anger 64

Anger Management: What Is It? 96

Reasons To Be Angry 108

Why You Must Seek Solutions 123

Understanding Anger 136

Anger Management Through Meditation 154

So Feeling Anger Is Not "Bad"?

"Anger is an acid that, when spilled, can damage the vessel it is held in more than anything else. Mark Twain

Anger has positive and negative repercussions, just like every other emotion we experience. Since anger primarily serves as motivation, it is not always negative.

Letting go of our anger allows us to relax and clear our heads to view the matter from fresh angles.

Anger motivates us to do better. For example, feeling upset at being ignored would motivate us to work even harder to accomplish our objectives and receive our due respect. Furthermore, the ability to contemplate anger is a reliable indicator of unfairness.

Anger is a transient diversion that helps us stay grounded throughout our darkest moments.

However, we must remember that none of these advantages are possible if our anger is out of control. Anger management is essential to reducing anxiety and raising the risk of depression. Hurried decisions and damaged sentiments also cause good partnerships to end. Lastly, anger negatively impacts our health—it harms our heart, lungs, and even our sleep cycle!

People who struggle with controlling their anger frequently don't stop to think. They need to reflect on times when they feel better, OR someone needs to talk to them about the issue to identify it. Regardless of the situation, you can determine whether you have anger management problems by responding to the following questions:

1) How often do you lose your temper?

If you respond daily, move on to the next inquiry, as there's a slim possibility that your ire is justified. Saying something more than once a day is already cause for concern! Individuals don't become upset too often! And inquire further: How long does my rage last?

2) What makes you angry? + Consider the causes of your anger. You may be experiencing anger management problems if minor and unintentional things irritate you. Nonetheless, your ire might be warranted if your work entails managing individuals, some of whom give you ongoing hassles. The main thing to remember is to ask yourself: Is my rage appropriate for the circumstances?

3) What state are your interpersonal relationships in?

Observe how other people behave around you: do they deliberately avoid you or approach you easily? Think about your friends: are they still asking for the monthly dinner, or have they already cut you out?

4) When did you last lose your temper and destroy something?

We frequently throw or break things out of anger. If this is something you do frequently, you may have anger management problems.

5) When was the last time you did or said something hurtful?

An individual with unchecked rage frequently says and does cruel things, and occasionally, they even turn abusive. When was the last time you told someone something cruel? Have you lately injured someone physically? Or was there ever a time when you almost hurt someone? If you can identify these circumstances, you must begin controlling your anger; if not, you will continue to suffer, and so will those around you.

To be fair, responding positively to these questions does not automatically imply that you are without hope. Half the fight is already won if you are still in a place where you can see that you need to improve. While some individuals with anger management problems require medical assistance, others only need to step back, think things through, and attempt some solutions.

After you've determined that you have anger management problems, you must identify the causes of your desire to suppress your feelings. Generally speaking, managing your emotions and resentment will improve your general health, but to be more precise, the following are the transformative advantages:

Improves channels of communication. You can stay in communication with individuals when you don't yell at them or hurl incoherently.

You'll have improved decision-making skills. You will regret your actions if your wrath prevents you from thinking rationally. Making decisions while furious frequently leads to hurried behaviors, such as verbally or physically abusing someone.

Your relationships will be closer and healthier if you have clear channels of communication and improved decision-making abilities. This is a result of your loved ones being comfortable approaching you.

Greatly lessen your stress. Being angry and not knowing how to stop yourself is a common heavy load that leads to stress. You may live a less stressful life when you can control your emotions and learn how to stop worrying. And this will be beneficial for both your physical and emotional wellness.

Develop your likeability. An angry individual is unlikable and unlikely to receive any kind of favor, no matter how tiny. Any profession needs authority, but likeability is just as important. This is beneficial for maintaining excellent ties with your coworkers.

Realizing these advantages will significantly enhance your life at work and home. If you can acquire these gems, the work you will put in to master your emotions will be well worth it.

The Distinctions Between Responding And Reacting

your responses to objects or people in your immediate environment have shaped a significant portion of your existence. most of these responses are not the greatest ones to take, and as a result, we wind up upsetting ourselves, other people, or both. some even worsen the circumstances.

without thinking twice, we say the first thing that comes into our mouths. our tendency to get defensive and respond quickly exacerbates the situation. instantly, we decide what to buy without even considering if we have the money to pay for it. these everyday occurrences show how frequently we behave without first thinking, especially when angry.

your response stems from an instinctive feeling brought on by fears and insecurities. usually, this isn't the most sensible course of action. responding is the opposite of reacting; it entails assessing the circumstances and choosing the best course of action in light of collaboration, compassion, and rationality.

discover how to react

it's commonly believed that if you speak out of rage, you'll say something you'll regret forever. the fact that you can never take back the words you utter emphasizes how important this remark is. you will feel so much worse once you have poured out your nasty on someone else's face, even though it is uncomfortable to sit down with your misery, frustration, disappointment, grief, and fury. you must develop the ability to control your anger and emotions to do this.

one can cultivate this internal pause by practicing mindfulness and living more in the moment. it calms down the natural response because being mindful allows you to live in the present moment, which creates such inner peace and calm that you won't lose your cool when someone lashes out at you. instead, you'll be more understanding of other people's mistakes.

by pausing, you give yourself time to process the information or action before responding. your inner voice tells you what you would normally say, but if you allow yourself a few moments, you'll see that the hurtful thing you would have said was unnecessary and wouldn't have made a difference in the first place.

i'm sorry to apologize. i detest having to get on my knees and beg for pardon. i feel like i'm adoring the other person when i swallow my ego and ask for their forgiveness. i developed this mindset as a result of making too many mistakes. when my temper got the better of me, i would spew whatever poison i could find in an attempt to make the other person feel as inferior and looked down upon as i had been made to feel. being quiet and collected by nature, i would automatically respond to hurtful comments with my own words, even if they were spoken softly.

after that, my conscience would not let me leave. following my outburst, i would engage in a never-ending internal struggle until, with my tail between my legs, i would apologize to the individual who had upset me. i hated this so much that i had to devise a fresh plan. i decided to hold off on becoming angry or reacting.

these days, if someone hurts me and i want to lash out, i stop dead in my tracks when i realize i have to go through the awkward process of begging for forgiveness. along with taking in what has been said and done, i also think about the possible outcomes. during those brief moments, i realized that i don't have to respond in kind and have the chance to act honorably. sometimes, you have to detest something sufficiently to wish to alter your actions or behavior.

the following actions can be taken to start the internal pause.

1. identify the triggers.

recognize the feelings that progressively accumulate within you, signaling the onset of irritation and anger. it could be a tight chest, knotting in your stomach, pulsing in your head, or a rising body temperature. you must instantly initiate your internal pause as soon as you recognize these as indicators that your anger has been aroused.

simple awareness and understanding of what is happening will cause your temper and ego to return to their source when you are embroiled in an argument and see that they are blazing.

2. pause: to complete this step, mentally hit the pause button while using the tv control.

3. inhale deeply: having a lot of oxygen in your brain helps you focus and collect your ideas. it also helps you become aware of the present moment.

4. look around: you should listen to others instead of rushing into

conversations or voicing your opinions. you do not need to respond immediately to anything you disagree with. simply jot down whatever thoughts that come to you; don't let any of them consume your time. for instance, if your objective is to cut back on your spending, think back to a goal you established or a slogan you came up with for a similar circumstance. consider the best outcomes as well. what outcome would you like to see in this situation? once more, permit yourself to carefully examine every thought going through your head.

5. now "play": it's time to take action now that you have considered every possible course of action for this issue, both good and negative. you must

approach this carefully. consider what kind, considerate, and wisest action you could take. what could you say to help everyone relax and find a better method to handle the situation?

although you might not initially be skilled at this technique, practice will make perfect. you will become more adept at halting; don't worry if you make a few mistakes. if you find yourself responding quickly, identify the feeling or idea that led you to do so, and be mindful going forward to make sure you can stop yourself from thinking that way.

you must be thinking that, although this procedure is too simple and effective on paper, it would not function in practice.

no one could mature through that long process in the heat of the moment. that isn't the case, though. for people with response issues, which is almost everyone, this technique has been tried and tested and found to be the best option.

yes, the procedure could seem lengthy, but if you have had trouble with inconsistent responses, it will help you recall how important it is to wait before responding. it makes a huge difference because it allows you to take a step back, determine what will work, and then carry on with your interaction in a way that makes you feel good about yourself and sets you apart from people who find it difficult to control their reactions.

The Dangers Of Getting Enraged

You will be acutely aware of these dangers if you have a short fuse and lose your temper easily. Being angry can be harmful; therefore, you should learn how to manage it. It is impossible to have a calm existence if you cannot control your wrath.

In this section, we'll show you how rage may ruin you, which should motivate you to study anger management techniques more carefully.

1. Experience friend loss

It has frequently been observed that furious people typically don't have many friends. Anger might lead to injuring your friends, which can isolate you and make you feel lonely. If someone is unwilling to control their rage, people will eventually have to put up with them. Anger can become even more destructive when you experience loneliness, which can be a serious issue.

2. Problems with blood pressure

It is also well-recognized that anger has detrimental impacts on your body. People who struggle with anger management have been seen to frequently have elevated blood pressure. Hypertension is the primary cause of many issues, so you should attempt to reduce it before it's too late. Many heart issues are directly related to hypertension.

3. Adverse force

Since anger is a negative feeling, it will inevitably make you feel quite negative. Regarding the notion of energy, you must comprehend where things are going. Your vibration will be negatively twisted if you are not contributing to enhancing your energy molecules, which will impede your total advancement. It will be difficult for you to switch between tasks, affecting your ability to pay attention and stay focused.

4. Despondency

Depression has also been observed to follow anger. Being excessively furious might make you irrational and frequently result in melancholy. Those with short-fused temperaments tend to keep things to themselves because they don't have many pals. A person who has few friends often feels lonely, which is the initial stage of depression. You must learn to control your anger if you want to escape depression.

Two types of depression can exist on their own. Depression that is self-directed might cause a person to withdraw and become a hermit. It's hardly ideal, but there is another type of sadness when individuals are perceived as being hostile.

These are a few risks associated with having anger management problems. You must control your anger issues and take care of business before it's too late if you don't want to fall victim to the same.

Now that you have the necessary basic knowledge of anger management let's look at some techniques to assist you in coping. Remember these principles the next time you want to give up on the anger management program; they should give you the much-needed motivation to press on.

Chapter 4: The 21 Everyday Techniques

People will inevitably encounter unpleasant situations, no matter how hard they try to avoid them. There will be stress associated with everything from an impending final test to getting ready for a trip, leaving for college, organizing a wedding, or purchasing a home. It need not, however, reach the point where stress consumes all of a person's thoughts. Even in impending stress, one can survive and perform well. People can learn some daily stress-reduction strategies from the part that follows. The advice may also be helpful to those who are searching for strategies to relax their bodies and thoughts due to anxiety issues.

#1 One of the most crucial actions to do when trying to manage someone's stress levels is to follow the first piece of advice. Ironically, when someone exerts physical strain on their body, they increase mental tension. Regular exercisers typically experience the biggest benefits from exercise.

According to studies, those who consistently work out have a lower likelihood of experiencing anxiety than people who don't.

Three primary factors contribute to this: confidence, sleep, and stress hormones. In terms of stress hormones, exercise gradually reduces a person's body's levels of stress hormones, particularly cortisol. Endorphin release can also be enhanced by exercise. These are bodily substances that positively reinforce an individual's mood. It's also a useful natural pain reliever.

Exercise has a beneficial impact on sleep quality generally. Thus, it can also have a positive effect on sleep. Exercise is a good technique to regulate sleep, as stress and worry can harm a person's sleep habits. People who use melatonin or other prescription drugs to help them sleep better amid stressful situations run the risk of becoming dependent on the medicine to get through the entire night. For this reason, physical activity is a beneficial substitute that may tire the muscles and soothe the mind.

Exercise can also increase confidence, so regular exercise might reduce stress levels.

When someone starts to feel stronger and takes care of their body, this transfers into feeling more self-assured. It's also likely that taking the time to exercise and make decisions about what goes into their body gives them a sense of control, which boosts confidence and has a favorable overall effect on mental health.

Picking an exercise regimen or activity a person enjoys is crucial when employing a stress-reduction strategy. An individual is more likely to come up with reasons why they can't work out on a given day if they select an exercise program they view as a chore.

Exercises that can be enjoyed include rock climbing, yoga, walking, and dancing. Additionally, research has demonstrated that stress-relieving activities like jogging and walking are particularly beneficial. This is so because the repetitive movements work the big muscles that consistent training strengthens.

Combining exercise with another soothing pastime is another technique to increase the enjoyment of the workout. For instance, A playlist of body-positive or motivating music can provide a mental boost to keep working out. Other ways to kill time include watching your favorite TV show or reading while riding an electric bicycle.

#2 Although taking supplements to manage stress may seem dangerous and unsettling, there are safe and helpful alternatives that might help. Green tea is one beverage choice. Antioxidants found in the organic supplement are beneficial to a person's body.

Because lemon balm helps to soothe the body and mind, it is associated with anxiety reduction. Because Valeriana can help with sleep, it's another alternative for stress relief. The supplement can calm the body, and the valerenic acid component modifies GABA receptors to lower anxiety.

Other alternatives for reducing stress include omega-3 fatty acids, ashwagandha, and kava due to their common ability to lower symptoms of anxiety and stress.

It is crucial to remember that some supplements may react negatively to specific drugs and create adverse effects in humans. For this reason, before using a supplement to lower stress, people must speak with a doctor.

#3 One can enhance their sleep patterns and lessen tension and worry by using essential oils or scented candles. Aromatherapy is the practice of employing scents to elevate one's mood and induce mental calmness.

Certain smells, such as orange, lavender, rose, neroli, sandalwood, geranium, and Roman chamomile, can calm a person.

#4 Reducing caffeine consumption is another method for lowering stress levels. All energy drinks, tea, coffee, and chocolate contain caffeine, a stimulant. The stimulant can induce tension and anxiety at high dosages.

Regarding the amount of caffeine that a person's body can withstand in a single sitting, each person has a different threshold. After consuming the stimulant, those with poor tolerance may experience jitteriness, shakiness, or anxiety. If so, you should think about reducing or giving up coffee completely.

Studies have shown coffee to provide health benefits, but these benefits are only real when the caffeine is used in moderation. It is best to use no more than five cups.

#5. Stressful thoughts have the potential to seriously disrupt a person's whole mental process. Put your anxious and tense thoughts in writing to stop this from happening. The alternative is to concentrate on listing the blessings one has rather than focusing on the difficulties.

Because thankfulness involves focusing on the good things in life, there's a chance that it can help people feel less stressed and anxious.

Seeing the good things in life can also help someone feel more confident in themselves, which can help them feel less stressed.

#6 Chewing gum is a quick, simple, stress-relieving activity you can do anytime, anywhere. Even studies showcasing the advantages of chewing gum have been carried out. One study revealed that chewing gum could make people feel more comfortable, reducing stress levels.

An additional research study discovered that chewing gum can strongly increase stress reduction. Gum can help reduce stress for two reasons: first, chewing gum produces brain waves comparable to those that happen when a person is relaxed. These benefits may seem unusual or difficult to believe. Another theory is that chewing gum improves blood flow to the brain.

#7 Ensuring that an individual has a robust network of friends and family members can serve as a solid basis for overcoming emotional and stressful adversities. In particular, participating in social networks can provide someone with a feeling of value and community.

A few investigations have examined the benefits of maintaining positive social connections. A study with a female focus was conducted. The findings showed that oxytocin, a hormone that the body naturally releases to relieve stress, is especially beneficial for women to have intimate interactions with friends and children. Strong support networks have also been proven to produce the opposite automatic reaction as the "fight or flight" response.

Men and women were the subjects of another study, which discovered that those with fewer social ties were more susceptible to mental health issues, including anxiety and sadness. The study also demonstrated the potential advantages of diverse social ties for both men and women.

#8 Allowing oneself to laugh is a fantastic method to reduce stress levels. Too much laughter makes it impossible for someone to concentrate on their worries.

A person can watch a hilarious TV show or movie, see a comedian they know would make them laugh, and surround themselves with family and friends who will accept them for who they are, which can all contribute to increasing their laughter.

Laughing can even help someone feel less stressed in a few beneficial ways. It can reduce a person's stress response, for example. Alternatively, a person's muscles can relax and release tension by laughing.

Long-term health advantages of laughter include bolstering the immune system and elevating mood. Another study that involved cancer patients had two sets of participants; one group received humorous relief, while the other did not. The test group members who had the opportunity to laugh at themselves had a greater ability to reduce stress than the persons who did not have this opportunity.

#9 It's not always easy to say "no" to people, despite how easy it sounds. When someone feels pressured to assist others, they may overextend themselves to the point that they cannot find time for their needs. Due to the difficulty in finding the time to complete everything that needs to be done might result in significant stress levels. It is imperative to remember that while many stressors are uncontrollable, others are. Among these is the ability to say "no" to others.

Being unable to say no to people can lead to a growing number of issues because when someone tries to manage too many things at once, they get overwhelmed and may start to doubt their ability to complete some of the assignments.

Being informed about the jobs one takes on and avoiding attempting to take on overly big loads of reasonable responsibilities are two ways to avoid taking on too many projects simultaneously. This will significantly reduce a person's stress levels.

Spend some time taking a step back and regaining control over the aspects of your life that you can alter, and that may be stressing you out. A person must first learn how to help oneself before being psychologically prepared to assist others.

#10 Procrastination has a few advantages, and the additional stress it can cause is not one of them. Procrastination has two main bad effects: it can make someone act compulsively or struggle to finish a task, and high-stress levels can create other health problems, such as poor sleep.

Individuals can control their stress when they can stick to their priorities and resist the need to put things off. Making a to-do list that helps one stay on top of everything one needs to do is one method to stop procrastination. Additionally, one can set their deadlines and make sure they are responsible for meeting them all.

It's a good idea to go down the list and set reasonable deadlines. Make sure to block out uninterrupted time for each activity and keep track of which ones need to be completed by a certain date. Trying to multitask and switch between different tasks might become exhausting.

Anger And The Controll Of Anger

The Nature of Anger: Many of you have really clear ideas about anger. We perceive rage as harmful and destructive. We believe that this is an improper response. We associate violence with rage. In short, we believe that anger is just wrong and that when we feel anger, there's a problem with us. Anger isn't a good thing. Anger is not a healthy emotion. Furthermore, anger isn't our friend.

Anger can manifest as any of these things. However, fury can also be helpful, necessary, and even healing. Our anger was necessary. All we need to do is learn how to express our anger in acceptable, thoughtful, and constructive ways. Anger is neither good nor bad in and of itself. It can be applied to cause harm or to bring about healing. While it might not be a very poignant emotion, it is nonetheless significant. We may all gain from revealing the nature of anger.

Anger results from unfulfilled expectations or from a communication that is not delivered. Anger is a tertiary response; our first feelings are grief and fear. Initially, we mourn the loss of the anticipation that was not fulfilled. We worry that nothing will ever change in the future. At last, we become enraged.

Thus, very few realize that anger may be a positive, healing emotion. Allowing ourselves to be angry sharpens our thoughts and fortifies our resolve. We uncover reservoirs of power and strength. By bringing about change, our alter gives us the courage and ability to dispel our fear that nothing will ever change.

Let us examine an example. We anticipate that people will respect our boundaries. When someone exceeds a boundary, that person's expectation is not fulfilled. First and foremost, we grieve the loss of the expectation that others will honor our boundaries.

We feel unsafe because our community has been violated. However, we also encounter fear. We fear that certain things will never change and that our boundaries won't protect us because other people won't respect them.

But what enables us to alter this is our anger. Our anger gives us the strength to stand up for ourselves. Our anger gives us the strength and courage to speak up and insist that our boundaries be upheld. In actuality, our anger makes us feel safe once more. Revealing our anger aids in refining and reinforcing our boundaries. We feel secure because we are aware of our ability to defend ourselves.

When we cannot express our anger in constructive, healthy ways, we believe nothing will ever change. We don't feel safe. Above all, we anticipate that we will never truly feel safe. Unspoken anger inevitably develops into bitterness and depression.

Our anger serves as a wake-up call. Our fury prompts us to become aware of a constraining belief. Owning our anger is the key to experiencing rage in a healing manner. After that, we can decide how to express our anger. We don't have to let our anger get the better of us or injure someone else. Rather, we can modify our perspective, alter the limiting beliefs, and rediscover a different aspect of ourselves. When we accept and comprehend the actual nature of anger, it might empower us and assist us in feeling completely safe.

What is anger?

Anger arises when we encounter a barrier in our pursuit of our objective. We confront such instances. We become upset and angry every day when we don't get what we want. Numerous psychological specialists, psychiatrists, and other medical professionals are addressing various psychological issues such as anxiety, depression, and other behavioral issues. They make an effort to assist laypeople like us. The layman must comprehend these daily conflicting situations and handle them skillfully.

Anger is a human emotion that is frequently expressed and can result in bad feelings, fear, and insecurity. Common societal issues include frustrations, fears, and disappointments that cause us to become more angry. We experience emotions frequently throughout our lives, and they significantly impact our actions. We must develop the ability to control our emotions; in particular, developing youngsters need to learn how to modify and alter their emotional expressions to fit their surroundings.

Anger arises every day. Life circumstances of women and the health issues they experienced, overcame, and developed. Many common problems, such as parent-child conflict, legal disputes, poor grades in school, child abuse, teacher-student violence, unmet expectations, and personal issues like anxiety, depression, and anger, may all be traced back to one common issue: anger. A layman is, therefore, confused with strangers from various backgrounds.

Understanding how alters develop in everyday situations and how to handle them is crucial. You can use methods for anger assessment to manage anger exploit. What are the main effects of the rage, how long will it last, why does it happen, what's going on in your body when anger flares up, and how does it advance in psychology? Common ailments include arthritis, cancer, diabetes, obesity, hypertension, and psychological issues (such as stress, depression, eating disorders, body dissatisfaction, legal conflicts, alcoholism, and drug abuse). Researchers have demonstrated that hypertilitность and argression, together known as the AHA-Syndrome, are associated with a higher risk of cardiovascular diseases.

Various personality traits include struggling with problem-solving, having poor memory, being afraid, not knowing what will happen, etc. The negative emotions will diminish our ability to govern ourselves. We refer to all of these negative emotions as internal factors.

What we refer to as external factors include inappropriate professional practices, traffic jams, waiting lines, heavy traffic, media and advertisements, social status, social anxiety, and so on.

Our rapidly evolving, technologically advanced, modern lifestyles and competitive businesses constantly challenge us. Positive emotions no longer have the same meaning. Terrorist assaults have made us feel threatened and insecure all the time. Even still, these days, we are more afraid of governments than of terrorist acts. Numerous negative emotions are merging into a single emotion. Furious.

For school-age children, anger is a common emotion they encounter daily. Kids carry firearms in their school bags. Events reported by students are covered by news outlets worldwide. Girls can be just as angry as boys, according to reports. They are known to retreat, shove, slap, bite, and strike when confronted with fear, particularly when it is fueled by envy.

That's why controlling your anger is essential at every stage of life.

Overview
Anger: What Is It?

"Physiological and biochemical changes, like other emotions, accompany anger.

Both internal and external events can spark anger. Your anger may be caused by worrying or being fixated on personal matters, a traffic jam, a plane cancellation, a particular person or event, or a combination of these may bring it on. Experiencing unpleasant or distressing memories can sometimes incite anger in someone.

Anger is being demonstrated by reacting angrily in the instinctive, natural way that anger is communicated. Strong, frequently violent feelings and actions are sparked by anger, which gives us the strength to defend and fight back when we are assaulted. Anger is a healthy, instinctive reaction to threats. Thus, we must be angry to some extent to survive. However, there are limitations to how far our fury can take us due to laws, social norms, and common sense. We are, therefore, unable to physically react to every person or object that irritates or frustrates us.

People use a variety of conscious and unconscious strategies to deal with their feelings of rage. The three main tactics are to be silent, inhibit, and express no. The greatest way to handle anger is to confidently and non-aggressively express it. You must learn how to make demands and comply with them without causing harm to others if you want to do this. It's necessary to be firm without becoming hostile or demanding if you want to respect other people and yourself.

Anger can be channeled, converted, or contained. This results from putting your anger aside, suppressing it, and focusing on the positive. You should learn to control or repress your rage to use it for constructive endeavors. Your wrath may turn inward and towards you if it isn't allowed to find a release outside of you.

Silent anger might give rise to other problems. It can cause pathological bouts of wrath, such as passive-aggressive behavior, which is when someone attacks someone without a reason, or it can cause a person to be angry and cynical all the time. Those who constantly make fun of others, criticize everything and say cynical things cannot manage their anger constructively. It is hardly surprising that they are unlikely to have many satisfying partnerships.

You can now calm down inside. This means controlling your behavior on the outside and your inner responses, lowering your heart rate, finding serenity, and letting go of feelings.

Controlling your anger

You can't eliminate or change the things or people that annoy you, but you can learn to manage your responses.

Section I

Anger: What is it?

Anger is defined in so many different ways by so many people. Whatever your term, we will all agree that anger is an emotional state that ranges in intensity from moderate irritation to extreme rage and fury. Physiological and biochemical changes, like any other emotional feeling, frequently accompany anger. Stated differently, an increase in heart rate, blood pressure, and the production of energy chemicals such as noradrenaline and adrenaline characterizes anger.

Many things have the power to enrage us. These events may occur within or externally. For example, you might be upset with a coworker at work for not turning in tasks on time, or you might be stuck in traffic and get a call informing you that your flight has been canceled. In other situations, stress and anxiety about a personal matter, such as recollections of a tragic incident like rape, might set off sentiments of fury.

So how can we express our rage then? Being violent is, after all, the most innate and natural way to show rage. Keep in mind that becoming angry is just a normal reaction to danger. When we are attacked, these feelings of rage give rise to a stronger, frequently aggressive emotion that enables us to defend ourselves by fighting. Put another way, to survive or deal with the current circumstance, we require a specific level of rage. Nonetheless, there is a contrast between controlling our emotions and snapping at anything or everyone that irritates us that most people overlook or fail to distinguish.

Even though your child hasn't cooperated with you at home, you shouldn't use your anger to vent to everyone at work because something else upsets you. There are a lot of things that can enrage us, but laws, societal standards, and common sense frequently have a significant impact on how far our anger can go. Some people cope and deal with anger by employing conscious and unconscious strategies. You must always keep three essential strategies in mind: calming, suppressing, and expressing.

The greatest approach to expressing anger is to respond healthily by choosing to communicate your sentiments in an authoritative rather than an aggressive way. If you want to do this, you must develop the ability to articulate your requirements and your plans for meeting them. I say this because it's critical to ensure that you are not causing harm to anyone while attending to these needs. Being aggressive and demanding is not a must for being assertive. It simply implies that you must be proactive and show yourself and others respect.

Conversely, repressing anger only results in its conversion and subsequent redirection. This is frequently the case when you decide to suppress it to shift your focus to something more constructive and stop yourself from thinking about it. Being able to channel your anger into something more useful rather than harmful is the fundamental goal of learning to repress your anger. Even though it could appear effective in the short run, this can be deadly. You may hold that fury inside and use it against yourself. Some people develop high blood pressure, depression, or even worse conditions as a result of their anger.

You must realize that there is risk involved in holding your rage inside. It might trigger additional, more significant issues. Put another way, you can develop a pathological expression of wrath. Rather than addressing someone directly, some people prefer to avenge themselves indirectly and covertly. Studies reveal that individuals who enjoy disparaging others, critiquing everything that happens to them, or even uttering inane remarks cannot effectively channel their anger. These folks frequently don't have fulfilling relationships.

At last, you can control your inward rage. This indicates that you are in charge of your internal and external responses. By doing this, you may ensure that you control your heart rate by just slowing down and letting your anger eventually go away. You have access to all of these methods. But if none of the three are effective, something or someone will suffer severe injuries, and you should be afraid!

Different Kinds Of Anger

Your heart thumps. Your blood clots. Red is what you see. You must yell. To make contact with something. To strike a hard object.

It doesn't feel much better because we've all been there. You're upset.

However, specifically, what sort of rage would you say you are?

Managing our anger, however, can be difficult if we cannot identify it or even lack the words to express our feelings.

You may be surprised to learn that there are numerous varieties of anger.

Understanding how to distinguish between the many forms of rage is crucial.

But the more you can identify the rage you are experiencing at any particular time, the more adept you will be at handling it.

Furthermore, if you realize this, it will be easier to regulate your anger and stop you from doing something you'll later regret.

Continue reading to discover the 17 distinct forms of fury so you can recognize your own.

1. Bold Fury:

An effective way to convey rage is through assertiveness. Assertive anger is delivered calmly. Aggressively expressing their rage requires them to control their impulse and find a solution.

Rather than retreating from a conversation or becoming easily agitated, assertive anger is a healthy and constructive approach to expressing discontent that leads to constructive change.

Assertive anger can seem like a wonderful, safe method to express your feelings. For example, you could start an assertion with, "I feel angry when..." or, "I believe..." along with appropriate nonverbal cues and, occasionally, preconceived notions on figuring out or addressing the situation. This allows you to vent your resentment in a way that encourages improvement.

2. Anger Driven by Fear:

There are times when being upset is easier than being afraid. That is especially clear when we fear for a friend's or family member's safety.

The people closest to us are the ones who can harm us the most. So, instead of expressing our concern when we witness them acting in ways that occasionally potentially harm them, we could react in wrath.

Furthermore, rage often leads to temporary, to some extent, outcomes. Intentionally or inadvertently, we may take out our frustrations on a loved one to shock them into changing their frightening behaviors.

However, it is counterproductive to express rage when our true emotion is fear.

Anger outbursts are hardly the best approach to protect the people we love from the things we fear for them; instead, they only cause harm, dread, and hatred in those we love.

3. Behavioural Anger: Men with anger management disorders often exhibit behavioral rage as a legitimate reaction. This can be dangerous since it can be violent and turn into terrible, uncontrollably angry feelings.

Anger behavior is ostentatious and erratic, leading to bad legal or interpersonal outcomes.

Behavioral rage can manifest as aggressive or frightening actions (such as shoving or tossing objects, chasing someone, or cornering someone and shouting your voice). Recognizing whether your anger is spilling over into this space due to potential legal or interpersonal repercussions is critical.

4. Dangerous Fury:

Although little research has been done on this kind of anger, findings about the outlandish culmination of behavioral fury are typically anticipated. This could involve being incredibly petty or even making fun of other people, even if it's not warranted.

When upset, they may use words or physical acts to harm others (such as throwing or smashing something important to the person they are furious with). This is known as destructive rage. This can occasionally appear in a relationship as stagnating or inwardly shutting away your soul mate. Destructive angerDestructive anger can negatively impact many aspects of your life, even to the point of destroying important social relationships.

5. Frustration-based rage: This type of rage resembles fear-based anger when directed at a friend or member of the family.

We have the highest expectations and the best standards for the people we care about the most. When we witness someone falling short of what we believe to be their greatest potential, we become irritated, and this dissatisfaction tends to repeatedly explode into rage.

Similarly, anger based on frustration can be controlled from within. Maybe we've become discouraged by life. Maybe we believe that others possess the things we lack.

While we struggle, going from one disappointment to the next, we observe as others seem to prosper.

The main foundation of this kind of rage is comparing your fantastical vision of how you believe life should be against how it is or looks.

But the reality is that life can never live up to your vision, whether for yourself or your friends and family.

Frequently Asked Questions on Anger

Is Getting Enraged Okay?

Anger is normal and even healthy. Being furious is a healthy way to deal with the cruelty you've received from those who have wronged you or any injustices you've encountered. We will all get furious at some point in our lives, but how we choose to handle our anger and recognize what makes us angry counts.

Never repress your anger because it's a bad emotion; instead, allow it to flow naturally so that you can recover swiftly. But remember that you should use caution to avoid overreacting, as this could cause harm to you or others around you.

Conditions in Which It Is OK to Feel Furious

If it inspires us to take action

Any time we experience anger, it may motivate us to take certain steps that hopefully result in favorable results. For instance, it can be risky to be in an abusive relationship. Anger can lead you to end the connection, averting potentially fatal consequences on the road.

If it increases our chances of surviving

Our fury will drive us to take defensive measures against attackers or predators that threaten us. We can either defend ourselves or run away. Some people are so fearless when angry that other people or predators have no choice but to flee in fear.

If letting go of your resentment calms

Tension leaves our body when we let our anger simply flow out without suppressing it. This soothing release usually settles the nerves and lessens the discomfort. This explains your composure following an outburst.

Your fury will only get stronger if you don't let it out.

Most of the time, suppressing your anger and not finding a way to let it out will just make it rot. As a result of the anger persisting, you can begin to despise the person who incited it, become ill, or perhaps have much worse outcomes.

If it aids in problem-solving

We become irate whenever we believe something is preventing us from getting what we deserve or want. Thus, it would be beneficial if becoming enraged inspires you with solutions to the issue so that you can achieve your goals.

If it forces you to reach your objectives

We will likely become angry when we don't get what we want. In summary, this could help us identify any weaknesses we may have, motivate us to work harder to overcome the obstacles in our way, and ultimately assist us in reaching our objectives.

If it can influence those in our immediate vicinity to behave differently for the better

We get upset when someone mistreats us, violates our rights, or takes advantage of us. Anger will alert us to the presence of an issue. Additionally, it can inform others that their actions are wrong. As a result, they may feel guilty for their actions and decide to alter their conduct.

If it encourages hope

When we are angry, we choose to ignore the suffering that our abusers have inflicted and instead concentrate on the good things in life. Anger motivates us to improve the situation by bringing forth some positive energy.

In negotiations, the irate win.

The negotiator who is furious has a greater probability of winning an argument when the two are trying to agree. For cordial relations, the opposing negotiator will be prepared to make concessions. As a result, fury can be a useful negotiating tactic.

If it results in constructive self-change

Anger has the power to reveal our flaws and weaknesses. For instance, if we identify the things that irritate us, we may focus on resolving them, enhancing our relationships and overall quality of life.

How much time does anger last?

It is best to take all reasonable steps to avoid harboring long-lasting anger. Dr. Jill Bolte Taylor, a neuro-anatomist, claims in a publication that anger ought to endure no more than 20 seconds! It will be said to you by others that you ought to be able to calm down physiologically in twenty minutes. The gender difference in anger duration is also evident. According to research, women tend to hold their anger within longer than men; this difference may be due to how men vent their rage.

We replay the things that made us angry repeatedly in our minds, which is why we get angry for extended periods. It shouldn't take long for us to give ourselves some alone time to let our anger out, depending on whoever we are upset with. This is because harboring resentment is equivalent to ingesting poison and hoping the person who harmed you would perish. These are a few tried-and-true techniques to assist you in letting go of your rage.

Recognize the cause of your rage.

Examine the source of your rage and the things that make you angry. Analyze the cause to determine whether it is something you can manage or beyond your control. If it's a family member or a coworker, calmly and directly communicate your anger.

Develop emotional self-control.

Practicing relaxation techniques is one strategy people take to manage their anger. You can handle anger more skillfully if you have mastered some of the most effective relaxation techniques that may help you relax anytime you are upset over anything or someone. You can relax by engaging in techniques like breathing in and out.

Take a little break.

Give yourself room to be alone if you are having a heated disagreement with someone. When we argue, we frequently say hurtful things out of anger, which might damage our connection with the other person. It is wise to leave and give yourself some time to cool off before returning later when you feel at ease.

Understand how to deal with pressure.

We can become highly agitated and furious very quickly as stress levels rise. Walking and running are two excellent physical activities that can relieve stress. Another well-known benefit of exercise is the release of endorphins, a hormone that reduces stress.

Find a way to stop doing whatever makes you angry.

Once you identify what irritates you, you can determine the most effective strategies for handling it. Consequently, you can direct your efforts into altering the circumstance rather than concentrating on your hunger.

Don't harbor grudges.

You will be at peace with yourself if you attempt to forgive the person who wronged you rather than harboring resentment. This will lessen any resentment and fury you may be feeling. Recall that you are a master of your emotions.

Speak with someone.

You can always discuss your feelings with a trusted person. When you are under a lot of stress, it can be helpful to talk to a buddy. The other person needs to be able to hear you out without passing judgment. Talking to someone might sometimes help you let go of your anger.

WHAT AM I INTENDING TO MANAGE?

You may have heard that controlling oneself is the main goal of rage. But with our fury, what are we attempting to control? To cease experiencing pain, we are attempting to take control of the cause of our suffering. Allow me to clarify. Anger is never the primary feeling. It reacts to the main emotions (see How Can I Deal with It for a list). For instance, Mark got upset when a storm postponed his plans to go golfing on his one day off. His main agony was disappointment and dissatisfaction. His ambitions were being obstructed, which is why he got upset.

Pain is always the initial cause of anger. People (apart from a medical issue) do not become furious without a cause. Many variables, including prior experiences, perception, interpretation, and coping mechanisms, influence why a certain main pain triggers in one person but not another.

Mark is in charge of how he vents his rage and attempts to take charge of his pain, disappointment, and frustration.

He must decide whether to control his fury or allow it to rule him. These are some possible responses that Mark might have.

He can be self-pitying and whiny, saying, "This always happens to me! It's always destroyed whenever I get an opportunity to do something enjoyable! He might vent his resentment on those in his vicinity. Even the smallest irritation can cause him to lose his cool with his daughter. Maybe he'll give her a hard time for not tidying up after her mess from a week ago in the basement. When she enters the room, he may start arguing with his wife about anything irrelevant to his main discomfort.

Mark might also decide to control his rage constructively. He can acknowledge his main source of pain, which is his extreme frustration at the way things did not work out the way he had hoped. He can move on from the setback and not let it spoil his day. He can arrange other plans. He can look bright and make the most out of the circumstances. "Perhaps this is a good thing. In any case, I really should be getting around to finishing a couple of things. I now have the chance because of this. I can still enjoy myself today. I am happy that I have today off. I'll be grateful and happy about it.

The amazing thing about healthily managing primary pain is that it deflects, attenuates, or eliminates anger's potentially harmful effects. Our unresolved rage no longer affects or controls our decisions, moods, or attitudes.

Some of our deep-rooted primary pain is triggered more frequently by long-standing unresolved concerns related to our primary pain. Leah, for instance, is insecure and highly sensitive. She has experienced rejection and mockery from her peers since she was little. Her expressed rage turns destructive when her primary pains of hurt and humiliation are provoked. Leah may believe that people dislike her due to her past experiences, and she may anticipate rejection. She may think she's unlovable and hates who she is. Sometimes, Leah might take something spoken as an insult to herself. For instance, Leah assumed that a coworker's disagreement with her concept meant that she didn't like her. Leah experiences primary pain of hurt and shame, which causes her to get enraged with herself. She might get nausea or headaches. Alternatively, she could turn to booze and drugs. To effectively address deeply ingrained primary pain, professional assistance may be required.

Chapter 2: Managing Your Fury

In the previous chapter, we delved into the anatomy of rage and addressed several important issues surrounding this sometimes misinterpreted feeling.

We've seen that anger is a basic human emotion and talked about the different types and how each manifests differently. To better control your anger, we'll talk about the significance of comprehension in this section and how to quickly identify the source of your rage.

This chapter will cover several topics, such as the origins of anger, how it affects relationships and your health, and how to become conscious of and accountable for your anger. By the time you finish reading this section, perhaps you will better understand your anger and know how to deal with it when it comes up.

Assess Your Anger by Asking, "Why Am I Angry?"

You're probably aware by now of how powerful an emotion of anger can be. This feeling can profoundly alter our perceptions of both ourselves and other people. Anger can harm one's job, relationships with others, and health if it is not managed. Given this, people must develop better-coping mechanisms to manage their irritation and rage. To do this, though, a thorough analysis that addresses the underlying cause of the issue is necessary.

When learning how to properly manage anger, the first step is to determine what is causing the anger.

● Events in Life

Anger frequently develops accidentally as a reaction to difficult, unforeseen life situations. For example, you will probably become angry if someone tries to pass you at a dangerous angle while driving on a highway. In fact, because of traffic, people who commute by car to work are more likely to become angry and frustrated while driving than at home. Road rage is a term coined to describe the widespread anger associated with traffic. This is simply one instance of how experiences in life might exacerbate anger management issues.

● Cognitive Styles

An individual's thinking may also factor in anger management issues. Anger is a secondary emotion that typically signals a fundamental emotion, such as fear, as we covered at the beginning. Consequently, fear-based cognitive patterns may be more likely to affect someone others have let down. They might be concerned that individuals will keep disappointing them. They could also lack trust because they highly doubt other people's motives. If these ideas are not challenged, they will soon turn into angry and frustrated thoughts.

● Action Sequences

Many people who struggle to endure frustrations never really learn constructive coping mechanisms for when they become angry. Rather than finding healthy outlets for their anger, they could hold their resentment inside and choose destructive methods to let out. This frequently develops into a pattern of irrational behavior, exacerbating their predicament. When anger consumes all of their identity, they might not even be aware that they have an anger management issue. However, by addressing the underlying cause of their anger through counseling and therapy, they can break the pattern and improve their anger management skills.

For this reason, as soon as you become aware of anger management issues, you should review the tactics you have been employing up until now. This will assist you in determining whether your coping mechanisms are functioning well.

You might need to ask yourself the following questions:

● Does my present approach improve or worsen my circumstances?

Let's say you got into a furious dispute with a friend, and to vent your frustration, you chose to cut off communication. You need to assess if giving yourself the silent treatment is helping you manage your anger or if it's only straining the relationship more.

● Has my approach previously proven effective?

It might be prudent to assess the efficacy of your previous anger management techniques. This will enable you to assess its success rate and decide if, given your current circumstances, this would be the best course of action.

● What more coping mechanisms are at my disposal?

Among the techniques you could use to manage your anger are:

Expressing your emotions to those in your support network, such as friends, family, spouse, kids, etc.

- Having faith in your ability to control your anger and in yourself

Taking Part in Activities for Self-Care. To feel better, you can want to treat yourself to your favorite chocolate or take a soothing bath.

Since thinking patterns and anger are frequently correlated, assessing some of our thoughts when we are furious is critical. A few of these ideas may not be beneficial to the circumstances. They might even make it impossible to see the true source of the issue.

Thus, the following are some things to consider when assessing your anger:

- This is not how I should be handled.

I'm unable to put up with this emotion.

I have to back up my claim.

Everyone intends to harm me.

- Nobody can relate to me

I had to let my frustration out.

When these thoughts start to creep in, you may identify the source of your anger more quickly and precisely by carefully examining them.

Anger Management: What Is It?

What Is Anger?

"An Emotional expression that shifts in force from gentle bothering to extreme fierceness and fury" is how Charles Spielberger, Ph.D., a clinician who studies anger, defines anger. Similar to other emotions, it is accompanied by physiological and biological changes. For example, when you lose control, your heart rate, blood pressure, and the amounts of your energy hormones, adrenaline, and noradrenaline all increase.

You might be angry at a specific person (a manager or coworker, for example) or event (a plane being delayed, a traffic jam, etc.), or your outrage might result from worrying or tormenting over personal issues. Angry memories of terrible or annoying experiences can also trigger angry feelings.

Why Control Your Anger

Anger can range in intensity from mild annoyance to extreme rage. Although rage is sometimes classified as a "gloomy inclination," it has a positive connotation.

Whatever the case, unchecked anger can lead to aggressive actions like yelling at someone or damaging property. Anger can also cause you to withdraw from the outside world and focus your outrage inward, negatively impacting your success and well-being.

Anger can be dangerous if expressed in harmful ways to one's physical, mental, or social development or if it is taken too seriously or feels too usual. Therefore, anger management techniques can be helpful and can help you find appropriate channels for expressing your feelings.

Why am I so easily prone to flying off the handle?

There are simple answers for our frustrations; if you explode, it can be the result of anything else you're going through, such as anxiety, fear, tension, financial difficulties, marital problems, or even coping with trauma. Hormonal abnormalities and temperament issues can both lead to outrage, as previously mentioned.

In any case, you may be wondering, How would I get less angry? You can employ many strategies to adjust to your outrage, even though change might not happen by accident.

Methods for Managing Anger

Studies consistently demonstrate the effectiveness of mental behavior mediation in managing rage. These medications can influence your thoughts and behaviors, among other things. They are predicated on the notion that your thoughts, feelings, and behaviors are inextricably linked. (Mental social mediations from anger management therapy are also demonstrated.)

Your thoughts and actions can either increase or decrease your emotions. You can alter your thoughts and actions to shift your emotional state away from anger. You will feel more at ease, and the fire within you will begin to fade without fuel.

Getting in the way of management control plans is the best way to regulate rage. After that, you'll know what to do if you get angry.

Chapter 2: Anger's Root Causes

Several things, including stress, problems with others, and financial worries, can bring on anger. Anger, for some people, is a sign of a more serious condition, such as depression or alcoholism. Anger is not regarded as a disease in and of itself, even though it is a recognized symptom of many mental health conditions. Here are a few things that might make you angry.

Depression

A mental disorder called depression causes persistent feelings of gloom, emptiness, and loss of joy. It is not the same as the mood swings that people frequently experience daily. Significant life events like a job loss or a death in the family may bring on depression. However, depression is not the same as the negative feelings one can experience following a difficult life event. Depression is characterized by strong, enduring feelings that are out of proportion to a person's circumstances and frequently persist despite changes in circumstances. This is a long-term problem, not a passing one.

Major depressive disorder is the most common type of depression, though there are others as well. It consists of bouts with symptoms lasting at least two weeks.

There are numerous ways that depression manifests. The following is a list of a few of the most common.

severe depression

A major depressive disorder patient is never joyful. They may lose interest in previous hobbies.

Disorders of persistent depression

Symptoms of persistent depressive illness, also referred to as dysthymia, persist for a minimum of two years.

depression following childbirth

The "baby blues" are a fleeting phase of gloomy or intense feelings that some new mothers go through. This usually goes away in a matter of days to weeks. Postnatal depression is a more severe variation of postpartum depression. There is no one identifiable cause for this type of depression, which can last for months or years. Anyone who feels depressed even after giving birth should see a doctor.

Significant depression with a seasonal pattern

Because there is less sunshine in the winter and autumn, this type of depression—formerly known as seasonal affective disorder, or SAD—often manifests itself. It might follow other seasonal patterns less frequently. It improves in response to mild treatment and during the remainder of the year. Those living in countries with long or severe winters appear particularly susceptible to this disease.

Anger can indicate depression, which is characterized by ongoing sadness and disinterest that lasts for two weeks or longer. Anger can be suppressed or shown overtly. Anger is expressed differently by each person in terms of its intensity and style of expression.

OCD, or obsessive-compulsive disorder

OCD sufferers engage in behaviors or ideas because of unwanted and repetitive thoughts, feelings, images, or sensations (obsessions); these behaviors are known as compulsions. Anguish results from not doing the compulsions, which an OCD sufferer frequently does to temporarily cease or diminish the intensity of the obsessions. Even while OCD varies in severity, if left untreated, it can negatively impact a person's performance at work, school, or home.

The following circumstances may include obsessions, compulsions, or both as part of the diagnostic criteria for obsessive-compulsive disorder:

Fixations

Most people define an obsession as a persistent, unwanted idea, urge, or image that causes them pain or suffering. The individual tries to suppress, ignore, or neutralize them with a different thought or action.

Obsessions

Recurring behaviors or thoughts that someone feels compelled to perform out of obsession or in compliance with strict guidelines are known as compulsions.

These obsessions or compulsions take up over an hour of the person's day or cause them to suffer or be impaired in a clinically significant way. For OCD to be diagnosed, the symptoms cannot be better explained by pharmacological side effects, by another mental illness, or by a medical condition. Anger is a common way that OCD presents itself, per a 2011 study. About half of OCD patients experience this. Anger can be a response to something or someone breaking a pattern or to frustration at your inability to stop compulsive behaviors and obsessive thoughts.

Reasons To Be Angry

Nobody knows for sure what generates fury. Anger is undoubtedly a human emotion, like love, hate, pleasure, sadness, greed, fear, surprise, patience, self-control, and so on.

Once more, just as with other feelings, what enrages one person might not outrage the person next door. Additionally, the effects of rage triggers can vary depending on an individual's age, gender, culture, or social standing.

However, some well-defined anger triggers can affect almost everybody to varied degrees of intensity.

In this tutorial, we'll focus on five elements that have contributed to the global persistence of the rage culture. Among them are:

parental illustration

The devastations of urban living

The unfairness slur

financial aspects

The impact of the entertainment sector

If you give these anger triggers some thought, you can see how your parents' example may have influenced what makes you angry, how living in small spaces can make you anxious, and how facing financial difficulties can frustrate you.

Unsuitable storylines for films, TV shows, and video games also tend to incite rage by portraying getting on other people's nerves as honorable, brave, and admirable.

Let's give the bullet points additional detail.

How a parent's example promotes rage

It was suggested to a young man in my neighborhood that he develop emotional self-control. "I cannot do so, even though I would love to," he shot back. My family is full of hotheads. My dad was always erupting like a volcano. He was my grandfather's son. It runs in our family.

You'd be happy to concur with him. It is a fact that your nurture may predispose you to rage. Your early surroundings, social group influences, and family can all impact how you respond to situations and problems as an adult.

People pick up on how to display anger at a young age by imitating the angry conduct they witness in others, according to renowned psychologist Harry L. Mills. This means that you'll be more likely to exhibit bad anger control as an adult if you were raised in a hostile environment where individuals frequently became angry over trivial issues.

Thus, if you currently struggle with anger, you may be carrying on a familial heritage. However, that does not imply that you will always be attached to rage, much like a fish on a hook. No. You can take charge of your emotions and take charge of your life. You don't have to give up control of your life to rage and stay in the passenger seat.

The devastations of urban living

You would note that city dwellers tend to be angrier than rural residents. You can see why this is with ease. In most of the most crowded cities on earth, traffic congestion is a major cause of stress.

The cities' noise, air and water pollution, crime, and police brutality are other sources of annoyance. Urban dwellers under stress are more likely to lose their cool and become enraged with one another over insignificant issues.

Despite how hopeless things may seem, you still have the power to decide whether or not to take offense at someone or something that bothers you.

You have possession of the key. And once you realize that rage is a negative energy that does no good, you will be committed to controlling your emotions, even when you feel like doing otherwise.

CAN I express my anger? - Things that make people angry

You're likely viewing "be happy" videos everywhere, learning to let go of your rage and never feel furious again. However, it is a fact that anger can exist sometimes. You also don't need to feel horrible. It's acceptable to feel angry and recognize that a certain emotion benefits you. Feelings like guilt, anger, fear, envy, and sadness are all important components of your "emotional intelligence." They are equally important as being content, joyful, and safe. You mustn't ignore or criticize your ideas because you think they're "bad" or don't think expressing these feelings is appropriate. As much as it is important to experience sadness and anger occasionally, it is equally important to experience happiness occasionally. It is a normal element of the flow of human emotions. The goal is to identify the causes of your anger, give your dissatisfaction some thought, and then select more constructive strategies to deal with these emotions. This is especially crucial for those raised in an atmosphere that does not allow them to express their anger freely or teach them how to deal with their feelings. If something is brought up, you could find it difficult to convey your frustration. You may not feel it, or you damage those around you and yourself when you overreact to rage.

The following justifies your right to feel angry:

It safeguards you.

Being able to express anger is a very useful talent. Suppressing your anger may result in you being unaware of unfair, insensitive, or coercive situations.

It spurs you into action.

Strong feelings about something might motivate you to take action and inspire you to make great life changes. For example, finding a better job may just require you to feel upset if you were employed in an abusive environment.

Denying your rage might lead to needless suffering.

Just getting furious will result in addictions, melancholy, and social isolation as you try to contain your fury. It may also cause you to lose faith and mistrust your emotions and sentiments.

Anger is a common feeling.

It is unnatural to think you can get by and never get angry.

Often, it's the initial stage of dealing with more complex feelings.

Often, anger is the first sign that anything is amiss. It's a clue that you must delve deeper to discover how you truly feel. Experiencing anger can also be a means of letting go of negative feelings from the past. Instead of addressing the underlying cause of the issue, you risk feeling unsettled or lost if you simply ignore your angry sentiments without giving them any thought.

Denying your anger could make you appear insincere or fake to others.

You can think of yourself as abnormally content and alienate people because they don't trust you.

Recognize and acknowledge your anger.

It's not always okay to be furious, as we sometimes say to ourselves when we become upset but fail to accept it. We may be angry at someone or the circumstance or simply not want to express it. One of two actions can be done if you're unsure if you're insane:

✓ Present the body. Register. Are you going to be very tense? Do you experience extreme bodily instability? If so, it might be anger of some kind.

✓ Determine the terms you use to characterize the experience. Or do you just mention that you're anxious? Do you mean that you're annoyed? We frequently use these words to describe our experiences, yet deep down, we are just angry.

Items That Set Off Anger

Feelings and thoughts are present. Feelings are present. Losing your cool, believing that your opinions and actions are unimportant, and inequity are just a few of the numerous factors contributing to growing irritation. Personal concerns and distressing or enraging occurrences are additional sources of frustration. The reasons behind wrath might also vary based on your expectations of others, yourself, and the environment. Your past experiences with anger constantly fuel your outbursts. For instance, you would either build up to an explosive outburst of rage or remain miserable if you were not taught how to communicate dissatisfaction. Inherited traits, brain chemistry, or health issues may also influence your propensity for the furious epidemic. Anger is a feeling that arises from how we see and react to certain situations. While each person has their own set of triggers, certain universal ones include situations in which we feel. Our minds might be stimulated in numerous ways, and these stimuli vary from person to person, depending on personal experiences. The symptoms are stronger when it comes to someone who controls or threatens you, for example, if you were threatened severely as a young person.

Here are some typical anger-inducing factors:

✓ Lying ✓ Relationship disputes ✓ Constant disappointment ✓ Lack of control, and ✓ Some persons, exclusively

You'll be able to respond to these stimuli more skillfully once you've identified them and started to grasp the trigger dynamics. Naturally, irritating feelings come on immediately, and you have to work hard to identify them and eliminate anything else you enjoy. For example, you were cut off while driving on the interstate. Note the physiological signals of wrath that alert you that you're angry. Take a deep breath and take a reasonable look at the situation instead of the first attack. Rather than assuming the driver you got cut off voluntarily (which may be your first thought), you would evaluate the chance that the other person might not notice you. It will be simpler if you understand that the disrespectful action was not meant directly to you or was an error. If you feel justified in your anger, you encourage yourself to get furious, whether it makes sense to feel that way. The more you stop rationalizing your fury, the sooner it starts to disappear. Although all your fury is real since it is the truth of how you feel during a given time, this does not mean you are always entitled to behave in your rage. Note that your fury is terrible for your health and detrimental to your crucial connections.

Why You Must Seek Solutions

As humans, rage is unhealthy and hazardous to our health and well-being. While an adequate level of rage could push us to make wonderful and life-changing decisions, an above-normal level of anger would undoubtedly destroy us both physically and psychologically. Wrath undermines our sense of normalcy and rationale, so we must seek methods to learn to control our wrath. There are so many reasons why we must seek remedies if we have determined that we have anger issues, and some of these reasons are;

1. ANGER CAUSES COMPLICATED HEALTH ISSUES. Refusing to learn to

regulate your anger issue results in health complications for you. You can have elevated heart rate, high blood pressure, and heightened adrenaline, which results in furious thoughts. Anger can also induce mental illnesses and other chronic ailments.

2. ANGER DESTROYS OUR PERSONAL AND NON-PERSONAL RELATIONSHIPS. The failure to regulate our anger makes our relationships with friends, family, and work colleagues suffer. Having angry and violent outbursts makes people cut their distance from you, and if it goes on, you will probably find yourself alone with a dead social life. Even more, rage might affect you in your workplace. When co-workers shun you

at work, it disturbs the spirit of teamwork, which must be present in any place of work. This leads to unproductivity and can make you lose your work. Even if you own your organization, it could scare clients and workers away.

3. ANGER MAKES US UNPRODUCTIVE. Being in a constant state of anger can make you unproductive because it puts your mind in a mess and withdraws your ability to think logically and cognitively.

4. ANGER IS SPONTANEOUS. The spontaneity of anger is another reason why we must seek to learn to control it. Anger can make you do anything without knowing what you are doing.

You usually only get to know what you have done after the anger dissipates.

5. ANGER IS A STRAIGHT AND DIRECT WAY TO SELF-DESTRUCT. Anger can destroy you emotionally, physically, financially, psychologically, mentally, educationally, and socially if you do not learn to control it.

6. FOR SOMEONE SEEKING LOVE, ANGER CAN EVEN MAKE IT DIFFICULT FOR YOU TO FIND LOVE. Because when people find out you are an angry and violent type, they will want nothing to do with you.

These are a few reasons why it is good to seek solutions to our anger before it destroys us. In the next chapter, we will discuss how to seek anger solutions.

Step 1: Practice Self-Acceptance

To treat any problem, you first have to accept it. If you fail to accept and acknowledge the issue, it becomes difficult to realize you have an issue that needs addressing. This makes you ignore the issue until it greatly exacerbates it. Since you do not want that to happen with your anger, and you instead want to save yourself from exploding with anger, you must accept yourself and your anger issues.

Self-acceptance is accepting yourself just as you are and making peace with all your issues. Self-acceptance helps you understand there is nothing wrong with being who you are. When you accept yourself, you start loving yourself, encouraging you to improve.

This realization motivates you to work on your anger issues and resolve them for good. To do that, you must be mindful of yourself and your anger. Here is how you can do that.

1: Be Mindful of Your Emotions

To understand if you have an anger problem, commit to a few weeks of being aware of your emotions and notice your behavior. This helps you notice the signs and symptoms of chronic anger. To do that, observe yourself very closely for at least two weeks, and always always have a pocket-sized notebook with you. Whenever you notice yourself exhibiting any of the following signs, write it in the notebook and explore it.

• Feeling constantly irritable • Losing your temper over trivial issues • Feeling constantly frustrated • Shouting or abusing anyone who angers you • Trouble understanding or organizing your thoughts • Thinking negatively about yourself or others • Not taking an interest in things you previously used to enjoy • Thinking everyone hates you or is against you

Keep a record of these emotional signs and symptoms of anger. If you regularly observe any two to three of these within the two weeks, you likely have an anger problem.

While you do that, also be aware of the physical signs and symptoms of anger, stress, and anxiety.

• Feeling exhausted without doing much work • Suffering from constant headaches • Nail biting • Experiencing pressure in the sinus or head cavities

While you can observe all these signs by analyzing your body, you must manually check your blood pressure using a blood pressure checker. Check your blood pressure at least twice a day; if it is around 120/90 or above, you have a high blood pressure problem.

To resolve that, it is best to consult your doctor. However, if you continue practicing mindfulness and the techniques mentioned in this book, you will also easily control your high blood pressure (hypertension).

2: Discuss with a Loved One

After observing yourself for a few weeks and spotting signs of chronic anger, discuss this issue with a loved one; this will help you confirm the issue with absolute certainty. Seek someone you trust completely, someone whose love for you is true, and engage that person in a discussion about the issue.

Tell your loved one you fear you have a severe anger problem, and it is likely the person will agree with you. This will help you validate your problem, accept it completely, and get the determination you need to treat it through mindfulness. Once you engage the trusted person in the discussion, ask the person to help you learn how to manage your problem and support you in the tough times.

3: Accept Your Problem

Once you have an anger problem, loudly and accept it. To do that, do the following:

1. Sit somewhere quiet and have your journal.

2. Go through the signs and symptoms of anger you recorded. This will help you understand you have a problem to manage.

3. Analyze your behavior, feelings, emotions, and quality of life and become fully aware of anger's negative impact on your life. Do you often stay unhappy? Do you find it hard to enjoy things you once

loved doing? Do you usually feel miserable? Is your work life and relationship suffering?

Ask yourself other similar questions and then analyze your answers. The answers help you understand the havoc anger is wrecking on your life.

4. Ask yourself if you wish to live a peaceful, happier, and serene life. This will help you accept that, like the people around you, those your anger negatively affects, you also want freedom from your anger.

5. Once you decide you are ready to escape your anger problem, accept and acknowledge it. Say, "Yes, I have an anger problem I need to deal with. From this day, I'll try to manage and resolve

this issue completely." You can create any other positive commitment you like.

6. Chant this commitment loudly, clearly, and slowly several times. Emphasize, "I need to deal with this, and from this day henceforth, I'll put in my best effort to manage and resolve this issue completely." The more you emphasize the positive words, the more committed you become to dealing with the problem.

7. Write it in your journal so you can solidify it.

By accepting your problem, you have taken the first step toward recovery. Congratulations are very much in order! The 'acceptance' phase helps you become more mindful of your feelings, emotions, and body as you pay more attention to yourself. Now that you are through with this step let us move on to the next chapter to find out what else you need to do.

Understanding Anger

Rage, especially rage that has been suppressed, ignited, or mishandled for extended periods, has been strongly linked to violent crime, as was briefly discussed in the preceding chapter. Violence is not a byproduct of mental illness, as Laura L. Hayes writes in her article "How to Stop Violence" for Slate.com. Furthermore, most violent crimes are not committed by regular, stable people who "break" out of their routines and become violent. People who cannot control their rage are the ones who commit violent acts. People with a violent past commit the majority of homicides. Murderers are rarely both mentally ill and regular, law-abiding citizens. The impaired ability to control one's anger results in violence.

These days, psychological disorders are far too frequently blamed for violent actions that make headlines or are identified as triggers. Although mental health issues are associated with a small percentage of violent crimes, the data indicates that this is not the case. Hayes refers to the numbers once more in her piece. "

Regretfully, there is a lack of emphasis on anger management when identifying the underlying causes of many crimes that persist in our society today.

Of course, this does not imply that someone who experiences fluctuating degrees of rage regularly is more prone to conduct violent crimes like murder or homicide. However, in many cases, in addition to the numerous potential triggers in the surroundings, past experiences, or psychological and emotional conditions surrounding an individual's response to angry feelings, the fundamental reason would also be a lack of comprehension and appreciation of the significance of anger management. How should you react appropriately? To handle anger responsibly, it would be essential to comprehend how it might influence your reasoning, thinking, and behavior. You must be honest about what triggers your anger and figure out how to deal with it head-on, whether by resolving it amicably or by preparing yourself to react appropriately when it does surface.

An appropriate grasp of anger control ought to start early in life. In her piece for Slate.com, Hayes states, "Chronic repressed rage that has no socially acceptable outlet fuels the violence that is a part of anger disorders." It is encouraged by households where adults exhibit intimidating, violent behavior or firmly suppress their rage. There isn't a suitable example of expressing rage constructively or safely in either scenario. Recently, there have been accusations that the mental health sector is not doing enough to help society deal with violent crime. I concur with this evaluation. We haven't done anything to stop the mindless violence surrounding people, and worse, we haven't offered a suitable diagnosis for out-of-control fury or a framework to help people comprehend it.

The good news is that if you're interested in learning how to control your anger and cope with it in your day-to-day interactions, many resources are available. Some experts can aid you with managing your anger, and strategies are continually being researched and refined to assist those who struggle to regulate their emotions. All you need to do is be prepared to take a close look at yourself, identify the source of the issue, and be receptive to suggestions for constructive change.

adverse consequences of fury

Determining whether the rage you are experiencing is "good anger" or "bad anger" is the first step. "Good anger" will support you in keeping cool and taking charge of your life, integrity, dignity, and limits. "Bad Anger" is when you become uncontrollably angry, damage those you love, and demolish everything positive around you. You have to learn to control your "good anger." Here are some indicators that your anger is becoming "bad anger."

You're not sure if your outrage was justified or not.

Once something enrages you, you can't let it go.

You lose control of your anger, which is uncalled for.

After neutralizing the issue, you are unable to relax.

And until you have a mental breakdown, your rage keeps building.

You frequently catch yourself losing your temper and mistreating others in your life.

Using filthy language and obscenities all the time.

Maintaining connections and relationships is difficult, and you frequently discover that people shun you.

You start abusing substances, booze, and narcotics heavily.

Impacts on your Emotional Health

Anger that is mishandled and destructive may and will disrupt your thinking. It will begin to change the very ideas that cross your head.

Depression: You are aware that you are angry, yet you are unable to stop yourself. You don't know how to manage your emotions healthily, and you feel powerless. You wait too long to discover that your anger interferes with your daily tasks, and you despair.

Paranoia: You begin to believe that everyone is against you, is plotting against you, despises you, and is speaking behind your back. As a result, you feel justified in responding angrily to everyone.

Brain Dysfunction: Anger leads to a variety of traumas, including stress and despair, which impair the brain's functionality. Focus problems, poor cognitive processing, memory loss, and other issues follow.

Adverse Impacts on Your Private Life

The most significant damage that rage does is to your interpersonal relationships. People constantly irritated will eventually come to avoid and break off communication with them. You might notice decreased spending time with your parents, siblings, friends, and spouse. Eventually, you can find yourself alone and trapped in an unending vicious cycle of shame, remorse, and rage. If you find yourself in this situation, you must act quickly to avoid pushing away all the important relationships in your life.

Which One Do You Think You Are?

Once you recognize your anger, you must learn to control it since it can destroy everything in your life. To determine if you can control it, you must first access how. Anger can be managed to some level, but it cannot be controlled once it reaches a certain threshold. Decide which rage style best describes you.

Avoidance of Anger

Even if you are bursting with tension and wrath beneath your grin, you intentionally deny being angry. You frequently hear yourself repeating, "I'm fine; I'm not mad." This type of rage is more accurately described as avoidance than passive anger. All you're doing is stuffing it deep within you and not dealing with it.

Why am I feeling this way about anger? You are conditioned from an early age to believe that rage is harmful, which is why you feel this way. You were forbidden from expressing your anger, and as an adult, you have been trained to suppress it by keeping it inside. Women typically fit into this group more since they are viewed by society as being calm, kind, and gentle. You would hide this while putting on a happy and peaceful front. You're unaware you can vent your rage constructively without using harmful force.

Anger that has been repressed can only be buried and suppressed so long before it explodes into complete pandemonium. To deal with this concealed rage, you can overspend, sleep too much, and engage in many other hectic activities. You must learn to speak up when something is wrong or disagree with anything someone is doing. If not, people will assume that whatever behavior they are projecting onto you is OK. People may tread on you unintentionally, but that's because you're not dealing with the problem when it comes up. Refusing to be angry in this way is practically guaranteed to destroy relationships.

You must first have faith that there are constructive ways to vent your anger to overcome this avoidance tendency. Assess whether you have a valid reason for being angry. Using reason, ask yourself whether or not what someone did was reasonable. Understandably, you would be upset if a coworker took credit for your work, and you should deal with this. Next, imagine a buddy of yours going through this. Consider your friend's reaction to this circumstance. If you put yourself in another person's position, you could discover that it is normal for them to feel angry and unhappy. Confrontation is the next step. You must get into the habit of letting out your fury as soon as it happens. Inform the person that you disapprove of what they are doing and that it is unacceptable. This will initially feel awkward, but it will get much less horrible and uncomfortable over time. You'll feel relief right away once you've spoken your mind.

A WONDERFUL NOTE ON ANGR MDNAGEMENT THNIQU

Anger is a common issue that many people face in their life. Even though everyone experiences anger, some people find it more difficult to deal with than others. For individuals who struggle with anger, several severe issues, such as road rage, addiction, or divorce, may arise. Fortunately, numerous effective anger management strategies can assist someone who is experiencing anger management issues.

Stress can be a trigger for rage. Thus, anger management frequently begins with stress management. Many people have extremely hectic and stressful lives due to their hectic work schedules and complex home or family lives. Understanding who you are and how much stress you can endure without becoming angry is crucial.

Developing empathy is yet another excellent strategy for stress management. This is attempting to see things from the perspective of another, as difficult as that may occasionally be. You might not be as quick to become angry with someone if you can learn to see things from their perspective instead of your own.

You frequently make unintentional or unpleasant mistakes when you react out of anger. It is crucial to learn how to respond to anger instead of just reacting to it. A more communicative approach is required when responding to anger, where you explain your feelings or situation before acting appropriately.

Moreover, disappointments can result in anger. If you anticipate too much or too little from someone, and things don't work out as planned, you could feel disappointed. Try to be more accurate in your expectations by adjusting them to work on this. Consider what you may reasonably expect from someone.

One of the most traditional—and still applicable—methods of managing anger is simply letting things go and thinking them out. This is still an excellent way to deal with anger since it eliminates unintentional behavior based on your reaction to becoming angry.

If you believe you or someone you know could benefit from assistance controlling your out-of-control rage, start by conducting an online search. You can also get assistance from a professional in your area, which may be necessary when anger becomes a major issue in a person's life.

Anger Management Through Meditation

One of the most effective methods you may employ to control any internalized anger or depression is meditation. It may be the true solution for your life's stressors, and doing less might infuse you with boundless energy. For the past three years, I have implemented this technique daily in my life and noticed a significant shift in my general happiness and how I handle situations.

I am among those who find it extremely difficult to stay grounded, particularly in the face of uncontrollable events.

Sometimes, I lose it, and when I reflect on how I behaved, I feel ashamed of how I handled the situation but also pleased that I could analyze it. Most people become irate, lose their ability to see their own mistakes, and place the responsibility on a diagnosis. It's not me; it's my rage problem.

The world's top leaders all talk about how they feel they have control over their minds because they meditate for 20 minutes daily. Anger and depression are more common among those who struggle to unwind and turn off their minds. I've studied meditation extensively throughout my life, and the main goal is to help you become present. Living in the present moment allows you to let go of all of your troubles and take a break from the never-ending struggle that is life. This will assist you in achieving peace of mind quickly if you believe you cannot do so.

Almost everyone I have spoken to has told me how hard it is to be present at the moment, particularly if you don't live there. I can assure you that you must think beyond the box if you wish to transform your anger into happiness. Try a variety of things to see what works best for you so that you can gain real-world experience. That's what allows me to speak about my experiences. I have experience with anger management; therefore, I am familiar with their precise mindset. For me, this has proven effective. You won't necessarily see results from it, but I'm confident your behavior will change somehow.

I started meditation to address my lack of social presence, and the transformation it has brought about over the past ten years is truly remarkable. Most people who practice meditation simply sit there, expecting that, eventually, their anger will subside. Your attention is diverted from your issues by simply being in the moment, observing the scents surrounding you, and noticing the air on your skin. Negative issues cause you to overthink everything and prevent you from being your best self since they cause you so much worry. It mostly prevents you from appreciating life and causes you to take everything for granted.

Because it improves your emotional condition, setting aside 20 minutes a day to simply switch off your brain can work wonders for your self-esteem. We act differently depending on our current state of mind and self-worth; for example, you would behave differently if you were excited than depressed. Like anything, I made a genuine decision about what I wanted and put it into practice, so my overall happiness shifted throughout the day.

Self-control is rewarding and leaves you with no regrets when you wake up five years later. Remorse weighs tons; discipline just ounces. I always give people a two-week test to push themselves to meditate for a particular amount of time each morning. By disciplining yourself to meditate, you'll feel like you're living because you're moving forward.

A person feels most alive and content when they believe they are making progress on something. I'll provide you with a meditation exercise so you can practice it right away and see the benefits.

Exercise for Mediation

1. Staying from the path is acceptable, but recognizing these moments and returning to your center is the key.

2. You can mentally repeat a mantra to maintain your attention on just one subject at a time.

3. Set a 15-minute alarm, and even if you want to give up, keep going; eventually, something will change.

www.ingramcontent.com/pod-product-compliance
Lightning Source LLC
Chambersburg PA
CBHW052138110526
44591CB00012B/1768